THE ASTROLOGY ORACLE

THE ASTROLOGY ORACLE

Your key to the secrets of cosmic guidance

Marion Williamson

All images courtesy of Shutterstock.

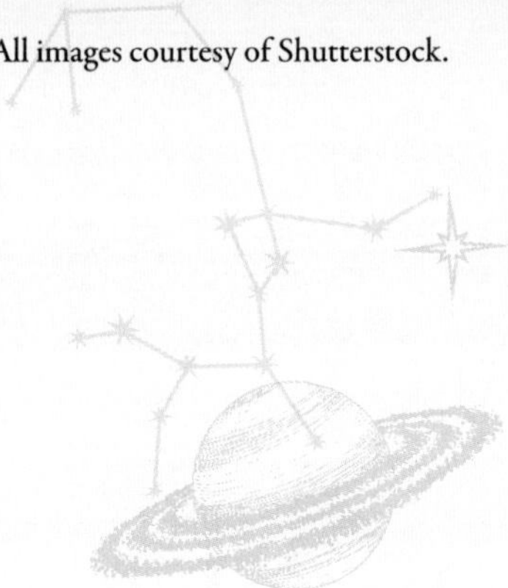

This edition published in 2025 by Arcturus Publishing Limited
26/27 Bickels Yard, 151–153 Bermondsey Street,
London SE1 3HA

Copyright © Arcturus Holdings Limited

All rights reserved. No part of this publication may be reproduced, stored in a retrieval system, or transmitted, in any form or by any means, electronic, mechanical, photocopying, recording or otherwise, without prior written permission in accordance with the provisions of the Copyright Act 1956 (as amended). Any person or persons who do any unauthorised act in relation to this publication may be liable to criminal prosecution and civil claims for damages.

AD012262UK

Printed in China

Contents

Introduction 7

Astrology Oracle Card Layouts 17
    The Lucky Trine 18
    The Challenging Square 27
    Elemental Spreads 37

The Card Meanings 75

Index of cards 128

Introduction

Welcome to your Astrology Oracle deck – an astrology-themed divination system that combines the ancient wisdom of the planets with transcendent alchemical symbolism and the timeless teachings of the divine goddesses and gods. These 50 beautifully illustrated oracle cards and this comprehensive guidebook offer an intuitive toolkit that gives insight and guidance on every aspect of your everyday life.

What is Astrology?

Astrology is the study of how the planets and celestial bodies affect our lives on Earth. Early humans marked the passage of time by observing the planets' intricate movements and patterns, as we still do today. The Sun's annual cycle through the zodiac and the Moon's monthly phases affect everything from the seasons, daylight, climate and sleep – a complex tapestry that shapes our lives in countless ways.

The life-giving force of the Sun was worshipped as the ultimate creator and the Moon's mysterious cycles were carefully recorded for their effect on rivers and tides.

Over thousands of years the meanings we have given the planets have evolved into the all-encompassing study of human experience that astrology is today. Offering profound insight into your personal motivation and behaviour as well as helping you understand your relationship with others, astrology teaches that everything is part of an interconnected reality.

Divine Beings

Astrological symbolism is as old as time, and our ancient ancestors saw the celestial bodies as divine beings – goddesses, gods or the spirits of long-gone predecessors.

The appearances of certain planets at particular times were attributed meanings that reflected the quality of nature we observed around us. As of course it has always done, the Sun, Moon and planets' positions change daily, monthly and yearly against their backdrop of visible stars. The days of the week were named after the Sun, the Moon and five of the visible planets, and were imbued with the characteristics of the goddesses and gods. The 12 astrological signs were born when the Babylonians divided the sky into 12 sections – each relating to a month of the year, creating the first horoscope or birth chart.

The planets were thought of as intermediaries between the human world and the spiritual realm, and somewhere in your distant ancestorial past you too would have looked to the planets for guidance, or to grant you luck.

Alchemy and Astrology

Alchemy is a Medieval practice that sought to turn base metals into precious substances, mainly gold. Mirroring the human quest for spiritual transformation, personal growth, and the discovery of one's inner gold, alchemists applied astrological timings, planetary correspondences with various metals, and planetary symbolism in their search for perfection. This interconnectedness between the cosmos and the material world was a fundamental principle in both alchemy and astrology, both of which were deeply rooted in the search for inner transformation and the quest to unlock the secrets of the Universe.

Your Astrology Oracle uses the same pillars and principles as the ancients, using only the planets you can see with the naked eye, and adhering to the mystical core of astrological and alchemical truths. Understanding these ancient belief systems can help you appreciate the interconnectedness of nature and your place in the Universe.

What is an Oracle?

We have used oracles for as long as we've been curious about the future or have turned to a higher power for spiritual guidance. Oracles come in many forms such as Tarot cards, rune stones and I Ching coins, and they all offer different ways of determining the future or guiding your intuition in the search for self-knowledge. The symbols and descriptions in your Astrological Oracle deck have been absorbed for thousands of years, and although some of their meanings have shifted to fit our modern age, they still have the same flavour they always had.

Your Astrology Oracle deck consists of 50 cards comprising 31 Astrology cards (7 Planets, 12 Zodiac Signs and 12 Houses), 12 Alchemical cards, and 7 Days of the Week cards.

Astrology Cards

7 Planet Cards

The planet cards represent the type of energy that is being expressed. As the planets are the main guiding principle in astrology, you will notice their repeating motifs and messages throughout the entire oracle, appearing in different guises through the personality type of the Zodiac Sign cards, the areas of life where the planetary energy is expressed in The House cards, as agents of change and transformation in the 12 Alchemical cards and their associated deities in the Days of the Week cards. The planets' symbolism and imagery will crop up many times in your readings.

12 Zodiac Sign Cards

The zodiac signs represent how the energy of the planet is being manifested and links to real people and personality styles you encounter throughout your everyday life.

12 House Cards

The astrological House cards relate to the 12 segments that make up the circular astrological chart, or horoscope. Each of these areas describes different aspects of your day–to–day life.

Alchemical Cards

The 12 Alchemical cards cover the planetary meaning of the alchemical metals and their planetary correspondences, and includes astrological phenomena such as comets, stars and the meanings of significant astrological points in a birth chart. The Alchemical cards are agents of change, and when they appear in your readings, they represent a shift in consciousness, a transformation of special significance that brings change, redemption, good luck and a chance to prove yourself.

7 Days of the Week Cards

Each day of the week is named after the Sun, the Moon or one of the five visible planets, and is also synonymous with a goddess or god. These cards offer advice and guidance, but they can also be literal days of the week when something significant occurs.

Your Subconscious Brings the Magic

This oracle deck is designed to open your subconscious mind. When you look at the pattern of the cards and read their meanings, you intuitively make imaginative assumptions about the story the cards are telling. Reading the cards acts as a bridge between your conscious and subconscious mind, so don't dismiss any unexplained or instinctual thoughts and feelings that stand out in your readings. These magical intuitive leaps arise from the vast sea of your subconscious knowledge, and give you a deeper, more personal insight into your readings, rather than just relying on the cards' literal meanings. Trust your intuition in any reading whether for yourself or others, as it's where the real pearls of insight spring from.

Upside Down Cards

In some oracle spreads, such as Tarot, the meaning of the card is reversed when the card is drawn upside down. That's not the case with your Astrology Oracle cards – the message is the same whatever way the cards land. Though if your intuition is telling you something isn't right with that card, it could be that the meaning is blocked in some way, and you can explore your reading with that in mind.

Oracle Spreads with Example Readings

The first part of your guidebook focuses on how to use the cards in specific spread patterns. Every layout is linked with an important astrological phenomenon: Trine (positive energy), Square (challenging energy), and the four elements used in astrology: Fire (action and passion), Earth (structure and practicalities), Air (intelligence and ideas) and Water (emotions and intuition). These are then followed by the card meanings that you can look up in the index on page 128.

Astrology Oracle Card Layouts

The layout patterns chosen for the Astrology Oracle are based on some of the most important astrological patterns and concepts: the Trine, the Square and the four element types: Fire, Earth, Air and Water. These represent the following energies: Trine (positive energy), Square (challenging energy), and the four elements used in astrology: Fire (action and passion), Earth (structure and practicalities), Air (intelligence and ideas) and Water (emotions and intuition).

Reading the Astrology Oracle for yourself and others
Three example readings are given for each layout type. The first reading offers insight into how you might interpret the cards for yourself, with a general example given that will help you understand how the cards work in that particular layout. The other two examples are of actual readings for other people, complete with their thoughts and responses to the reading.

The Lucky Trine

Each zodiac sign shares its element type with two other signs, and a trine pattern occurs when two or more planets share the same element. For example, if one planet is moving through the zodiac sign of Cancer and another is in Pisces, that's a trine. Trines are fortunate connections that show opportunities, natural talents, luck and harmony.

The zodiac signs that share the same element are:

Zodiac sign		Element Type	
♈	Aries	🔥	Fire
♉	Taurus	⛰	Earth
♊	Gemini	💨	Air
♋	Cancer	🌊	Water
♌	Leo	🔥	Fire
♍	Virgo	⛰	Earth
♎	Libra	💨	Air
♏	Scorpio	🌊	Water
♐	Sagittarius	🔥	Fire
♑	Capricorn	⛰	Earth
♒	Aquarius	💨	Air
♓	Pisces	🌊	Water

The Lucky Trine reading

When to use the Lucky Trine layout
Use this spread when you need a boost or want to be reminded of the good in a particular situation. The Trine spread is especially useful for supplying joyful inspiration during tricky times. This optimistic layout gives hope and reminds you to appreciate your blessings.

Layout Pattern
Lay three cards out in a triangle pattern: two on the bottom and one on the top.

Card position meanings:

Bottom Left Card
Meaning: Positives You Don't Appreciate
While shuffling your deck let your intuition guide you to the card that shows you where you can't see the woods for the trees. Or if you're reading for someone else, imagine you're in their position and looking for guidance. What is going on here that is being underestimated or undervalued? Make a mental note of any emotions or thoughts that come up, as they could be useful in your reading.

Bottom Right Card
Meaning: Action Needed To Realize Happiness
Allow your fingers to be drawn to the card that's going to help you, or the person you're reading for, to let go of things that aren't working, and to be open to new opportunities.

Top Card
Meaning: Likely Outcome If You Apply the Other Cards' Advice
Don't focus too much on what you want the outcome to be – just feel your way through the cards for their wisdom – rather than your own desires.

Your example Lucky Trine reading

Background

For your example reading imagine you have a set routine, a decent but uninspiring job with enough money to cover your bills and keep you afloat. You have a stable home life, good friends and everything is okay, but you feel it's time you challenged yourself or explore your potential. Can the cards help turn you in a new direction?

Your example cards

Bottom Left: Positives That You Don't Appreciate: *Saturn*

The Saturn card shows that you take your responsibilities and commitments seriously, but you can be quite hard on yourself, which makes it more difficult to appreciate your many talents. You might not realize that it takes you a while to make your mind up, or settle into a new routine, and you can be self–critical when trying something new. This reluctance to stray from your well–trodden path could mean you're a little anxious about your world unravelling or becoming too chaotic if you move too far from the practical, structured path you are on. The good news is that everything looks good for you to dip your toe in new waters because once you commit yourself, you respect your new ambitions and stick with them until you reach your goal.

Bottom Right: Action Needed To Realize Happiness: *Thursday*

The Thursday Astrology Oracle card is connected to Jupiter, the planet of luck and joy. This is one of the most fortunate cards in the whole deck and in many ways has the opposite meaning to the Saturn card. This optimistic influence shows that the action needed to realize your happiness is to expand your knowledge and experience through travel, learning and discovering new philosophies. Of course, Thursday could also be an important time when you see clues as to what will bring you the most fulfilment. A conversation or something you read about on Thursday could set you off researching interesting possibilities.

Top Card: The Likely Outcome If You Apply the Other Cards' Advice: *Quicksilver*

Quicksilver is an Alchemical card, which means a transformational shift is brewing. You may be shocked at how much your life will change when you take on the advice of the other two cards. You have amazing abilities to adapt to new circumstances, even if you feel that your life is a little restricted now. A few little changes need to be made so you can open your world to new possibilities. Don't doubt your talents, the Quicksilver card as the outcome shows you're bursting with good ideas. There's a whole other side of your personality to explore.

The Lucky Trine reading – Louise
(she/her), 25, Skelmersdale, UK

Background

Louise went straight from school into a catering job that she was employed in during the school summer holidays. She has friends there, but she's outgrown the job, and is thinking of applying to colleges and universities as a mature student. She would love to work in travel and tourism but is worried that retraining or going into further education will be unaffordable, or a waste of time.

Louise's cards

Bottom Left: Positives That You Don't Appreciate: *Gemini*

The appearance of any zodiac sign usually represents an actual person, not necessarily someone who shares that astrology sign, but a person who embodies the qualities associated with it. Gemini suggests a teacher, clever friend or mentor will guide Louise to appreciate her own capabilities and help her make up her mind. The presence of such a quick–witted card shows Louise likely has the intellectual skills and mental dexterity to turn her hand to any new subject, and, as Gemini is also linked with communication, education and language, a new start in the travel industry could be a real possibility.

Bottom Right: Action Needed To Realize Happiness: *Ketu*

Here we have the card associated with innate skills, things Louise is naturally good at but may not value because they just feel like a natural part of her personality. She may be worried about making

a move, but needs to appreciate her abilities, which will give her the confidence to take the next step. The Ketu card also advises against stagnation, which could mean that action needs to be taken to launch Louise into a more positive place.

Top Card: The Likely Outcome If You Apply the Other Cards' Advice: *Venus*

Venus is the planet of cooperation and harmony, showing that good relationships could be the result if Louise follows the other cards' advice. Part of Louise's question involved money and being able to work through her course, and the presence of Venus is a good sign that she'll be able to do this. As Venus is linked with hospitality and harmonious working relationships, maybe she could keep her current job part–time or seek a similar one to see her through university.

Conclusion for Louise

"I'm actually meeting a course administrator in a couple of weeks to discuss my options – including loans and financing. Maybe she's the Gemini. Talking to her on the phone did get me more excited about the course, especially the new language options, which is something I've always wanted to do. I loved Spanish and German at school, but I stopped learning when I left – the Ketu cards fits in with that, I think. I really don't want to take on a loan, and if I do decide to take the degree, I'd have to work my way through the course, so hopefully that Venus card is right!"

The Lucky Trine reading – Charli
(they/them) 37, Dumfries, UK

Background

Charli has not had a date for six months but would love to meet someone to share their life with. They have recently moved to a shared flat, have a stressful but enjoyable job as a designer in an advertising agency, and have a large circle of friends and a vibrant social life. But Charli feels no romantic buzz with anyone – what's in the cards?

Charli's cards

Bottom Left: Positives That You Don't Appreciate: *Mars*

The Mars card is bursting with fast–moving, hot–headed, sexy, and impatient energy. The positives that Charli may not appreciate is that the longed–for romance could be possible. Mars can show that a new relationship is coming, or that there are many people who find Charli attractive.

Bottom Right: Action Needed To Realize Happiness: *Caduceus*

The Caduceus Alchemical card shows something transformational is in the wings, which could be the action needed to realize Charli's happiness. This card's appearance describes a guardian angel influence, and also suggests that Charli may need to spend more time looking after themself or needs to make peace with the past and to be kinder to themself. Something's coming up for Charli that suggests their diplomacy skills could bring peace to existing relationships that will bring more happiness into their life.

Top Card: The Likely Outcome If You Apply the
Other Cards' Advice: *Sixth House*
The Sixth House card in this position wants
Charli to pay attention to their eating, sleeping
and wellbeing. This card's advice is to stick to a
healthy routine, tidy up loose ends and seek a
balanced approach to life. A new sense of order in
Charli's life could make more space for a new love
to flourish.

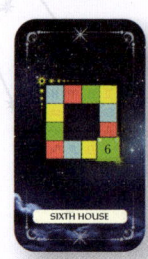

Conclusion for Charli

"That was so interesting because although I think I want someone
in my life, I'm also doing a hundred other things that I enjoy. I
don't know if I'd have quality time to devote to someone special,
but I do get lonely at times. And yeah, for sure I need to stick
to a less chaotic routine, and eat better… I'm basically living on
supermarket sandwiches and energy drinks. What was odd was
the diplomacy card – my mum's getting married to someone that I
don't really get on with, at least I didn't when I was younger, but I
never really gave him a chance. I see this reading as a sign I should
slow down a bit, look after myself, and then maybe I'll be more
ready to commit myself to sharing my time with someone new.

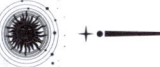

The Challenging Square

A Square pattern in astrology occurs when two or more planets are four zodiac signs apart. When a square occurs the energy of the planets is blocked, which results in tension and conflict. Squares aren't all negative though as their appearance also points to catalysts for growth and development. Zodiac signs that form Squares are:

Aries (Fire) squares: *Cancer* Water | *Capricorn* Earth

Taurus (Earth) squares: *Leo* Fire | *Aquarius* Air

Gemini (Air) squares: *Virgo* Earth | *Pisces* Water

Cancer (Water) squares: *Aries* Fire | *Libra* Air

Leo (Fire) squares: *Taurus* Earth | *Scorpio* Water

When to use the Challenging Square layout
If you're struggling to make something work, using the Square Astrology Oracle layout gives you a sense of what's holding you back or frustrating you. Squares become easier to deal with when you have a clearer idea of what's going on.

Layout Pattern
Lay four cards out in a square pattern: two on the bottom and two on the top.

+· THE CHALLENGING SQUARE ·+

Card position meanings:

Bottom Left Card
Meaning: The Problem
When you shuffle through your deck let your intuition guide you while you think about the challenge in front of you, or the person you're reading for. It's time to take a closer look at the barrier that's blocking or preventing you, or your querent from moving forward.

Bottom Right Card
Meaning: Who Can Help?
Imagine someone or something could make things better for you, or the person you're reading for as you let your intuition point you to the right card. This could be a person, an organisation or a group who can help you see more clearly.

Top Left Card
Meaning: Unexpected Resources
When searching for the right card, think about what could help you, or your querent, to make things better. Money, help, brilliant ideas or unforeseen circumstances could all make a big difference.

Top Right Card
Meaning: How You Can Change Things
While searching for the right card to help you or the person you're reading for, Keep your mind open for something that could magically materialize that would benefit the situation.

THE ASTROLOGY ORACLE

Your example Challenging Square reading

Background

For this example reading, imagine you have lost a friendship, a job, or a way of life that was very dear to you, and you're feeling a little hopeless and overwhelmed. You've chosen the Challenging Square layout to help you see why things are so difficult.

Your example cards

Bottom Left Card: The problem *The Moon*
Your feelings are at the heart of the matter. Deep feelings are present and maybe you feel like you're on an emotional rollercoaster. A strong attachment to someone could be both draining and wonderful, and you could even feel you're channelling someone else's sensitivities. It's a time to trust your feelings and instincts, even if they take you somewhere unexpected. The problem might be that you're grieving for your past, or feel flooded with strong emotions.

Bottom Right Card: Who can help? *The Comet*
The Comet is an Alchemical card representing something completely new and transformational. In this position The Comet suggests an individual, or a likeminded organisation could take you somewhere new and entirely unexpected. You can't see The Comet coming, and its effect could knock you off your feet a little at first, but once life settles down, you'll appreciate The Comet's magic.

Top Left Card: Unexpected resources *Taurus*
As Taurus is a Zodiac Sign card this may represent a person who makes you a surprise offer of help or who points you in the right direction. Taurus people are calm, patient and offer practical help – and they do anything for a quiet life. Someone with Taurus characteristics could turn out to be your rock if you're going through emotional turmoil. Taurus is also linked with money, so there's a chance of unexpected financial help, or a beautiful gift.

Top Right Card: How You Can Change Things *Sagittarius*
The Sagittarius is another Zodiac Sign card, so is linked with someone who reflects the Sagittarian qualities. This could be a larger-than-life character who makes you laugh, and helps you get your problem in proportion. This person could be determined to get you enthusiastic about life again and may inspire you to break away from current difficulties and explore something so utterly different that it at least takes your mind off your current predicament.

The Challenging Square reading – Jabari

(he/him), 42, Bourges, France

Background

Jabari has been with his partner Kai for seven years, and they have been very happy together. They both have time-consuming careers and recently they bought a home together. Out of the blue Kai confessed he would love for them to adopt at least one child. Jabari assumed they were happy as they are and has never thought of starting a family. Can the cards shine any light on his situation?

Jabari's cards

Bottom Left Card The Problem *Gold*

Gold is a card of abundance and accomplishment, and in the position that explains the heart of Jabari's problem, it's an intriguing card to work out. Jabari may feel like he has the perfect relationship as it is and doesn't want to introduce more changes.

Bottom Right Card Who Can Help? *Friday*

Friday is linked with Venus, the bringer of harmonious relationships, love and friendship. This is a lovely card see in this part of Jabari's reading because it means he is probably surrounded by good people with fair advice. The Friday card could also mean an independent stand should be taken, and maybe that's the advice he will hear – possibly even on Friday as the weekday cards can also represent the day someone helpful could make an appearance.

Top Left Card Unexpected resources *Eighth House*
The Eighth House card symbolizes beginning and endings, and being at an exciting crossroads, which seems appropriate for Jabari and Kai. This card's message is that Jabari may have more power over the situation than he realizes, as the Eighth House is extremely strong and resourceful and could advise that Jabari's resources are one of his strengths. Kai may not even want to go forward with adoption if Jabari is not fully on board.

Top Right Card How You Can Change Things *Seventh House*
This is a lovely card to see in this position and its appearance means Jabari has love and support on his side and whatever his decision, the outcome will be in his favour. The Seventh House suggests his relationship with Kai is strong, and that the people round Jabari want to please and are keen for a harmonious resolution.

Conclusion for Jabari

"I realized during the reading that I assumed having a family would be bad for our relationship, because we're so happy together, and kind of selfishly, I think, introducing a child into our world would mean we're less part of each other's lives. I'd thought one of us would have to stop working too, but although I still don't feel it's the right time for us, we really haven't talked about it in detail. I had a knee–jerk reaction and got a little carried away – I'm not even anti–adoption. It's made me wonder if these feelings are even my own. My father has strong views on the subject – maybe I'm just parroting him."

The Challenging Square reading – Ellie

(she/her) 19, London, UK

Background

Ellie recently left school and didn't do as well as she'd hoped in her exams. Most of her friends have moved away to college or university, and she misses them and feels left behind. She's not excited about what lies ahead and is harsh on herself about not getting the grades to have kept up with her friends. She lives at home and wants to find a job that will help her find her feet and make a new life for herself

Can the Astrology Oracle Pack point her in the right direction?

Ellie's cards

Bottom Left Card: The Problem *Sunday*

Sunday is a card that sheds light on any circumstances, and the problem for Ellie is that she can't imagine her next step. The Sunday card speaks of increasing popularity and creativity, and reminds her that she is much more resourceful than she might realise. Maybe she isn't giving herself enough credit to fully imagine who she wants to be. And of course, something may happen on Sunday that crystalizes the nature of her problem – or could be a catalyst in how she moves forward.

Bottom Right Card: Who Can Help? *First House*
With the First House card in this position, it points to Ellie being able to help herself. This is a card that asks Ellie to look at her own personality and how she is expressing herself. She may find that either it's a lack of confidence, or that she may be comparing herself unfavourably to others without good reason. A fresh start is on the cards if she can reimagine herself and has the self-belief to give her own talents and desires a chance to be realized.

Top Left Card: Unexpected Resources *Fifth House*
The Fifth House gives further strength to Ellie bringing her talents to the fore. Surprise resources come from Ellie's own interests and hobbies. She also needs to enjoy her inner child-like qualities. Ellie needs to get used to being herself and the chances are that she'll receive flattering attention if she does. Love, romance and fun are in the cards, and existing partnerships become even stronger. She's probably being too harsh on herself and needs to discover more about what she likes and dislikes – then life could take an unexpected upward swing.

Top Right Card: How You Can Change Things *Regulus*

The Regulus Alchemical card shows the brilliance of Ellie's potential. This overall reading is overwhelmingly in her favour, showing that her own talents will take her where she needs to go if she follows her joy. Sometimes it takes courage to be wholly herself, but this card shows that Ellie could be at the top of game if she becomes more self–reliant. Making responsible decisions are important now too, but Ellie's headed for greatness if she answers her calling.

Conclusion for Ellie

"This really rang true for me, especially the First House card about comparing myself to others and not really focusing on what I really want. I feel a bit lost, but from this reading I see I need to really think about what I love doing or what inspires me and to head in that direction. I've always loved fashion and have made a couple of dresses. I enjoyed doing it but was put off the idea by a teacher saying I wouldn't make any money from it. Maybe I could prove her wrong. I'm going to trust my own judgment and sail by my own star from now on, especially if that Regulus card has anything to do with things."

Elemental Spreads

The Elements
Astrology is based around the elements of Fire, Earth, Air and Water, and each zodiac sign is linked with an element type.

Fire Signs: Aries, Leo and Sagittarius
Associated with passion, energy, and creativity.

Earth Signs: Taurus, Virgo and Capricorn
Grounded, practical, and focused on the physical world.

Air Signs: Gemini, Libra and Aquarius
Intellectual, communicative, and socially oriented.

Water Signs: Cancer, Scorpio, Pisces
Emotional, intuitive, and deeply connected to the subconscious.

The following four Element spreads are themed depending on your query, or the nature of the question someone else would like the cards' advice on:

Fire layout is best for:

Useful for asking for guidance on: travel, exploring, passions, new ideas, adventure, taking risks, sport, sudden changes, spontaneity, enthusiasm or burnout.

Earth layout is best for:

Best for giving guidance on practical matters such as money, home, health, work, getting organized, buying a home, luxury items, treating yourself or food.

Air layout is best for:

Questions based around communication, conversations, education, what people mean, learning, being adaptable, intelligence, short journeys or siblings.

Water layout is best for:

Queries about: feelings, love, connection, relationships, intuition, emotional security and insecurity or emotional wellbeing.

•+ ELEMENTAL SPREADS +•

Elemental Fire reading

When to use the Fire layout

You will benefit most from an elemental Fire reading when passions are high. If you or the person you're reading for is angry, frustrated and vengeful or passionate, intense and enthusiastic, the Fire layout will work best. Feelings are loaded, and ready to explore, but it's probably hard to see what's in front of you objectively.

The layout comprises a column of four cards laid out in a vertical line (see left).

Card position meanings

Bottom Card
Meaning: What Lit the Fuse?
Let your fired-up emotions, or those of your querent, choose a card while thinking about what created those heated circumstances. Let your higher self be attracted to the card that sums up the problem.

Second Card
Meaning: What Added Fuel?
What has contributed to this situation feeling so intense? Ask yourself or the person you're reading for to think about what has kept this fire to burn so brightly. What's feeding the emotions in this situation?

Third Card
Meaning: Do You Want to Stop the Fire?
Ask yourself, or the person you're reading for to think about whether there is pleasure in the warmth of the fire or is it too hot to handle and making you uncomfortable. Is the feeling too intense or not passionate enough?

Top Card
Meaning: Illumination
What information will shed light on your, or the querent's, question? What needs to happen so the conclusion is clear? What kind of light needs to shine on these cards to give a satisfying conclusion?

Your example Fire element cards

Background

For your example reading, imagine you are angry with someone at work who is not pulling their weight, or taking their job seriously enough. Your colleague is very popular, chatty and likeable, but you're having to work doubly hard to meet deadlines and take care of business, which is making life more stressful. What insight do the cards offer here?

Bottom Card
Meaning: What Lit the Fuse? *Libra*

Libra is a zodiac sign, so we're dealing with a person here. Libra people are charming, sociable, fair and diplomatic. This card may represent yourself, the person you're reading the cards for, or the popular but lazy colleague. Whoever this card represents, Libra's dislike of conflict means it's already a good sign that there will be a happy outcome to this conundrum.

Second Card
Meaning: What Added Fuel? *Wednesday*

Wednesday is associated with the clever planet Mercury. Words of wisdom may come from fellow workmates, your boss or a loved one, but it's important to make sure you understand both sides of a story before you act. The Wednesday card can also be taken literally as when something will happen that crystallizes your, or the querent's, feelings on the matter.

Third Card
Meaning: Do You Want to Stop the Fire? *Taurus*
The Taurus card is associated with a person or people who either have Taurus as their zodiac sign or who share the characteristics of Taurus. Loyal and dependable with a dislike of emotional drama, this Taurus person doesn't want to make a big fuss or draw attention to the 'fire' in this situation. This is a good sign that nobody wants to upset the applecart, and that the situation will be settled amicably.

Top Card
Meaning: Illumination *Lead*
Lead is an Alchemical card of beginnings and endings. In this position, what brings light to your question could be revealed in a transformational change. Something will happen that makes your mind up. Sometimes Lead advises us to listen to someone more experienced – so talking to someone in a more influential position at work could help bring this irritating situation to a close. Lead also points to understanding the power of your own potential, so the changeable aspects of this alchemical card could see a surprise outcome. Maybe the person leaves of their own accord, or a new more exciting position could become a possibility for you or the querent.

ELEMENTAL SPREADS

Elemental Fire reading – Hannah
(her/she), 36, Stuttgart, Germany

Background

Hannah loves football and has been a player since she was a teenager. A knee injury means she can't play as much as she used to, but she's thinking of giving up her day job as a carer to retrain as a football coach or a physio and is keen to know if a reading can help her at this interesting turning point.

Hannah's cards

Bottom Card

Meaning: What Lit the Fuse? *Monday*

The Monday card is associated with the Moon, which shows fluctuations in mood and strong feelings, and the need to take care of others. Monday shows expressive talents lurking beneath any shyness. A need to stop daydreaming is also part of this card's influence and could be why Hannah suddenly feels motivated to make a change. Monday also could describe an important date in Hannah's diary.

Second Card

Meaning: What Added Fuel? *Friday*

Another weekday card, Friday is a people-pleaser card that wants to form harmonious relationships and keep people close. Friday could mean Hannah may need to stand up for herself more and shouldn't be shy about her opinions.

There's a dislike of conflict, but the enjoyment of the good relationships she cultivates with others is what's keeping her going.

Third Card

Meaning: Do You Want to Stop the Fire? *Tin*

Tin is a joyful Alchemical Card connected with optimistic planet Jupiter. A stroke of good luck could take Hannah to another level, where life unfolds, and doors that were once closed could open. Tin is a sign that she'll be pleased to keep her passion for football burning, and that surprising, transformative experiences could be on the cards soon.

Top Card (Fourth)

Meaning: Illumination *Leo*

Leo is a sign of the zodiac and therefore represents a person or people with similar characteristics. A generous friend, or someone she knows with boundless energy and creativity, could make her a pleasing offer. Leo is a passionate zodiac sign but it's also one that thrives in company. This all sounds positive for Hannah's wish to share her passion for football with other people.

Conclusion for Hannah

"I love my job as a carer which probably fits in with the Moon card being the thing that ignited me. Not long after talking to you I realised that what really gets me excited is actually rehabilitation – helping people to keep moving, and football's the obvious vehicle for me to do that. Not sure what Friday means yet, I'm no fan of conflict – I'm all about finding out what people need and helping them get to that point. I'm still waiting for the good luck from the Tin card, but I feel I'm getting closer to my true passion."

Elemental Fire reading – Raj
(him/he), 29, Leeds, UK

Background

Raj is an entrepreneur and drone enthusiast who has used drones to locate missing pets in the past. Raj asked the cards about his latest passion, which is in the early stages of development: a pet–monitoring drone service. What does he need to be aware of if he decides to turn his latest obsession into a working business model?

Raj's cards

Bottom Card
Meaning: What Lit the Fuse? *Pisces*

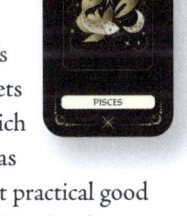

The Pisces zodiac sign card describes a person, or someone with Pisces attributes. Pisces people are compassionate, intuitive and empathic so Raj's enthusiasm for reuniting people with their lost pets could have come from a desire to help others, which could make him the Pisces. This sun sign often has wonderful ideas and a boundless imagination, but practical good business sense isn't usually linked with Pisces, unless they have an agent or someone to help promote their creative genius.

Second Card
Meaning: What Added Fuel? *Cancer*

Another person card, Cancer is a family card that values nurturing, feeling safe and supporting others. Someone close to Raj may be encouraging him to keep going, giving him more fuel to continue with his business project.

Third Card
Meaning: Do You Want to Stop the Fire?
Sixth House
The Sixth House card relates to hard work, attention to details and a scrupulously well–organized set-up. For Raj this conscientious card means does he want to devote all his time and energy to this project? If he's willing, then he can keep the fire burning but things may quickly fizzle out if he doesn't give this his full attention. This is not a project that will take off by itself.

Top Card
Meaning: Illumination *The Moon*
For the Moon card to provide illumination, Raj's emotions surrounding this new project are high. He may be feeling a bit sensitive about his abilities, and his hopes for success may have roots in his childhood. The meanings he's projecting on to the drone project may be more important than the practicalities, and the Moon is asking Raj to try to separate his own thoughts and feelings from those of the people around him.

Conclusion for Raj
"I'm not completely put off the idea, though I can see the cards are suggesting there's more practical work to be done, which is definitely true. The Cancer card was probably from my wife and son, who both love the idea. My wife and I work for animal charities and have adopted two rescue dogs and three cats, so we're passionate about pets and hate hearing of pets that have gone astray. That Sixth House card brought it home for me because I'm more about ideas and motivating people, rather than doing the nitty-gritty stuff, so I need to get that sorted. I take from the reading that I'll need a more practical approach to this."

•+ ELEMENTAL SPREADS +•

Elemental Earth reading

When to use the Earth layout
Earth layouts work best for practical concerns. Necessities like money, food, home and health are all Earth's territory, as is when you need to feel grounded, sensible and have some structure in your life. Use Earth spreads when you need common sense, a reality check or when you feel you're stuck.

Layout pattern
Four cards are laid out in a horizontal row (as below).

Card position meanings

Furthest Left Card
Meaning: Where Are Your Roots?
While you think of what you, or who you're doing the reading for, needs the Astrology Oracle's help with, leaf through the cards and see if you feel drawn to a particular one that might describe how the situation in question has evolved.

Left Middle Card
Meaning: What's Keeping You Stuck?
Even if you know exactly what's keeping you from moving, be optimistic that the next card will offer inspiring guidance on how you can wriggle free and move forward. Let the secrets of the Astrology Oracle reveal themselves as you feel for the card that will give answers.

Right Middle Card
Meaning: What's the Weather Forecast?
Now you're searching for a card that could make a prediction about what kind of conditions you, or the querent you're reading the cards for, will need to adapt to. Choose a card that help you adapt to any unexpected changes on the horizon.

Furthest Right Card
Meaning: How Will You Flourish?
Without focusing on any one scenario, let your hands intuitively find the card that has your, or the querent's, best interests at heart. Keep your heart and mind open to new possibilities as you feel your way through the pack for the card that will how to thrive in these circumstances.

Your example Earth reading cards

In this example reading, let's suppose you're frustrated at work because although you love your job and the people you work with, you just aren't earning enough money to make it work long-term, and want some advice.

Furthest Left Card
Meaning: Where Are Your Roots? *Friday*

Friday is named after lovely Venus, the planet that needs people around to feel happy, and works at making those relationships count. You've likely worked hard to achieve such close relationships with your colleagues and feel rooted, or attached to them. Friday may also be a time when something significant happens that makes your situation clearer.

Middle Left Card
Meaning: What's Keeping You Stuck? *The Sun*

The Sun is the card of creativity and life–living energy, so you probably feel popular and needed in your role at work. You may have a creative job that brings you joy, or what you do brings light and happiness to others. The powerful Sun card in this position shows it will be difficult for you to wriggle free from such enjoyable aspects of your position.

Middle Right Card
Meaning: What's the Weather Forecast?
Fourth House

The Fourth House card is one of family and nurturing. This caring card asks you to look to your childhood for reasons you might be in these specific circumstances, as old anxieties could come up for re-evaluation. Working from home may become an option soon, or you could discover a moneymaking sideline that you could do outside of your normal working hours that may supplement your current income, and let you hang on to the job that's so hard to drop.

Furthest Right Card
Meaning: How Will You Flourish? *Mercury*

If you are truly doing what you love in your current job, the flexibility of the Mercury card suggests you could stay there, but that it would be a good idea to diversify your interests. Mercury always finds a way to move, and the cards are telling you that if you seek new ground, you will solve your problems. It's time to be more Mercury – ask around, make inquiries and email people in the know. Mercury also suggests that juggling more, smaller jobs could be an enjoyable way forward.

• + ELEMENTAL SPREADS + •

Elemental Earth reading – Kenny
(he/him) 48, Philadelphia, US

Background

Kenny moved to the US when he was in his twenties and is now settled in Philadelphia as a science teacher. His mum, Joyce, lives in London and they both wish they could spend more time together since his dad died seven years ago. Kenny wants to know if the cards can give him any advice, as he likes where he lives, and his family are settled, but he is also very close to Joyce and wants to lend more support where he can.

Kenny's cards

Furthest Left Card
Meaning: Where Are Your Roots? *Third House*
The Third House asks Kenny to consider how he expresses himself to others, and them to him. Communication listening and analyzing are important – and when applied to Kenny's roots, this could refer to his role as a teacher. As Kenny's mother is a key part of his question for the cards, this 'roots' card feels as though it may naturally relate to his relationship with her.

Middle Left Card
Meaning: What's Keeping You Stuck? *Jupiter*
Jupiter is one of the happiest cards to see in any reading, and in this position could relate Kenny's enjoyment of his work and his life abroad. Jupiter is linked with travel, philosophy and new cultural experiences, which seems to tie in with his life and family in the US, where he has an enjoyable lifestyle.

Middle Right Card
Meaning: What's the Weather Forecast?
First House
The First House card turns up when a fresh start is on the cards. Kenny will likely undergo a period when he discovers a new way to relate to the people around him. This could refer to how Kenny's mother becomes a more influential part of Kenny's daily life. Kenny may review his strengths and weaknesses and this may impact how he feels about his own self-image.

Furthest Right Card
Meaning: How Will You Flourish? *Silver*
The Alchemical Silver card shows that a transformational change is ahead. Silver relates to self-reflection, contemplation and self-care. Associated with the Moon, Kenny's feelings may be magnified around his mother, and the decisions before him. As Silver is in the 'flourish' position – Kenny's emotions about this situation will lead him to make the right decisions. A more logical, practical approach isn't likely to help, so Kenny is being asked to follow his heart.

Conclusion for Kenny
"The reading made me feel quite emotional. Both my parents were also teachers, which the 'roots' card definitely picked up on. I'm not sure about the 'weather forecast' card as it shows a change of image, but I've not quite decided what to do – I have thought about coming back to the UK for a while, and even investigated a teaching position, but it's complicated! Video calls aren't the same as seeing someone in person, and I miss her. How I interpret the last card is that it's telling me to follow my heart, which I know is driving me to be nearer to her – just not sure how yet!"

+ ELEMENTAL SPREADS +

Elemental Earth reading – Jax
(she/her) 25, London, UK

Background

Jax is a doting single mum trying to make ends meet. Her family are supportive of her and her four–month–old daughter, Kayla, but Jax graduated with a degree in film studies and is determined to find a way to use her videography skills to work from home.

Jax's cards

Furthest Left Card
Meaning: Where Are Your Roots? *Scorpio*
With the Scorpio card as her roots, Jax has a resourceful, tough, trustworthy person as her rock. Scorpio people are loyal, driven and clever, and this person could be Jax's anchor in life, a reliable source of wisdom and experience.

Middle Left Card
Meaning: What's Keeping You Stuck? *Caduceus*
The Alchemical Caduceus card tells of a coming transformation, and a time of healing and balance. As this card's main message is one of being looked after by a higher power during a tricky time, what's keeping Jax from moving on could relate to her lovely family, looking after her and guiding her through any challenges.

Middle Right Card
Meaning: What's the Weather Forecast? *Mars*
Mars means business and doesn't take no for an answer. A storm of activity or a sudden opportunity could be waiting in the wings for Jax, and things could escalate quickly. A card that demands action, Mars can be a hard taskmaster, and she'll have to respond quickly to get the most from the situation. Mars could also describe a passionate new relationship that takes her by surprise.

Furthest Right Card
Meaning: How Will You Flourish? *Thursday*

Thursday, the day named after Jupiter, is a lucky card that shows Jax her cheerfulness and fun-loving nature could be the source of the energy that will help her flourish. She's advised by this wise card to accept opportunities and push for bigger and better projects. Of course, Thursday could be an important day in Jax's calendar too.

Conclusion for Jax

"I'm actually a Scorpio – so maybe that 'roots' card is something to do with me. I'm a determined kind of person, but I couldn't do any of this without help from my family. I am kind of stuck, but in a good way. It would be lovely to get into a position where I could move out and be earning enough to look after myself and Kayla. I'm happy to see that Mars card – it gives me a boost because I'll need that energy in my spare time to showcase my skills, but a relationship is the last thing I need right now! I love that Caduceus card – a guardian angel looking after the pair of us – it's probably my mum! I can see that I need to move fast and make the most of any chance to get my films under the nose of the right people."

Elemental Air reading

When to use the Air layout

Use the Air layout when you want to know what's on someone's mind, or why they haven't been in touch, to find out which subjects fascinate you most, for inspiration when you need to feel excited about life or when you're bored and don't feel the energy you need to make any changes. Again, the first reading is given as general one for yourself. Remember to make a mental note of any feelings or thoughts that come up for you, or for the person you're doing a reading for, during the reading, as these could be insightful intuitive leaps that get to the heart of what is causing the block or could release any potential.

Layout pattern
Four cards placed in a diamond shape, as shown below.

Card position meanings

Bottom Card
Meaning: What's on Your Mind?
While you're looking to pick this card for yourself, or whomever you're reading the cards for, try to imagine the card that will sum up the situation you, or your querent, is in, and let yourself be drawn to the card with the most helpful meaning.

Middle Left Card
Meaning: What Is There Too Much of?
What's tipping you, or the person you're reading the cards for, over the edge? What needs to be held back or restricted to make this situation work better? Let your fingers pull you to the card with the answers.

Middle Right Card
Meaning: What Is There Too Little Of?
Now you're looking for the card that tells you, or the person you're reading the cards for, what there's not enough of. What needs to be encouraged to grow and what would nourish this situation?

Top Card
Meaning: The Perfect Balance
Somewhere in your Astrology Oracle deck is the card that will show how you, or the person you're reading the cards for, can find harmony in the situation that's before you. Tale a deep breath and clear your mind of any strong notions, and choose the card with the best advice.

Your example Air reading cards

Background

For the purpose of the following reading imagine you have a passionate crush on a friend who is sending mixed signals, and you don't know where you stand. You're not sure if they're happy being friends or whether your good relationship has romantic potential. What advice might the Astrology Oracle offer to help you through your strong feelings?

Bottom Card

Meaning: What's On Your Mind? *Aquarius*

As Aquarius is a Zodiac Sign personality card could describe someone who embodies Aquarian characteristics: rebellious, curious, sociable, quirky and unpredictable. Aquarius tends to be aloof and brilliant – an independent, friendly person who can be a little lost when it comes to dealing with their emotions. This card may describe the qualities of the person who has been on your mind, or could also represent someone who will come into your life soon.

Middle Left Card

Meaning: What Is There Too Much Of? *Twelfth House*

Mysterious and deep, the Twelfth House can be a beautiful but confusing place. This card tells you to trust your instincts, but it could be tricky to sort your real feelings from fantasy or to separate your emotions from those of the people around you. This card suggests there's too much illusion and not enough solid reasoning, so you may be projecting your feelings onto the person you have a crush on rather than seeing any clear reciprocation from them.

Middle Right Card
Meaning: What Is There Too Little Of? *Lead*

Lead is the Alchemical card of beginnings and endings and can be quite a tough card as it links with practical Saturn, the planet of hard work and reality checks. Too little Lead in your life means you need to pull yourself up by the bootstraps and listen to more experienced people's good advice. Alchemical cards promise transformation and give you a chance to experience an extraordinary shift, but Lead isn't a romantic card, so in this instance would mean the friendship you have is not the romantic fantasy you are hoping for. You may need more boundaries and a structure in place to help you move forward.

Top Card
Meaning: The Perfect Balance *Thursday*

The Thursday card is a welcome appearance as it reflects Jupiter's hope and optimism. The surrounding cards show that although the person you want to fulfil your romantic hopes might not come to anything, there's a happy outcome to your question. Fantasy and longing can point you to what's missing in your life, and jolly Jupiter can reorient you to a more fulfilling path. You have the wisdom and experience to turn this situation around for the better. Thursday may also be the actual day you hear or read something that inspires you to try something new, and travel is also linked with this fortunate card.

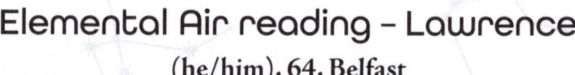

Elemental Air reading – Lawrence
(he/him), 64, Belfast

Background

Lawrence has just left his job as an aircraft engineer after working for the same company for 26 years. His wife, Kelly, is retired now too, and they are thinking of moving to Spain to spend long summers with their grown-up family. He and Kelly have a lively social life in Belfast, and he hopes to keep that up in Spain.

Lawrence's cards

Bottom Card

Meaning: What's On Your Mind? *Jupiter*

Jupiter is always a lucky sign wherever the card makes an appearance. Expansion, travel and optimism are the key themes, which fit with Laurence's hopes to make a new life for himself and Kelly. There's an extravagant aspect to the Jupiter card that puts worries aside and focuses on enjoyment. A willingness to learn about different cultures is also shown here, and a slight warning to keep an eye on spending, or of overdoing the good things in life.

Middle Left Card

Meaning: What Is There Too Much Of? *Sixth House*

The Sixth House card is associated with routines, work and habits. This could refer to Lawrence's time at work, what he's done enough of relates to sticking to tight schedules for many years and being very organized. The Sixth House is about being of service to others, which he probably feels after his 26 years in the same job.

Middle Right Card
Meaning: What Is There Too Little Of? *Iron*

Iron is an Alchemical card, so a change or transformation will be an important part of Lawrence's journey. Iron relates to the courageous planet Mars. If there has been too little Iron in Lawrence's life, this might refer to his desire to make brave choices, but the timing wasn't right, or he didn't have the resources to see his plan through.

Top Card
Meaning: The Perfect Balance *Rahu*

Alchemical Rahu points to a transformational shift forward, as this is the card pointing Lawrence toward something that both scares and excites him. His future is about to open in more ways than he can currently imagine. Rahu usually shows skills that you have to work at to reap the benefits, which means he may need to make an effort to be open and sociable, instead of relying on the friends and family he's known all his life. Rahu describes Lawrence's expansion of his comfort zone – new areas of life that feel unfamiliar, but exciting.

Conclusion for Lawrence

"That Iron card, and the Sixth House one are so accurate. It was hard to leave the job, and they didn't want me to go. I had great colleagues and worked for a company that treated me well, even if I was starting to long for another kind of life. It's been hard to leave the job behind, even though in my heart I know it's time to enjoy life and my family more, I struggled to make the decision. The Jupiter card sounds positive, so I'm going to embrace the future—and if that's an extravagance, so be it."

Elemental Air reading – Penny
(her/she), 47, Worthing, UK

Background

Penny and her wife, Kat, have a son Noah, who is finding his first year of secondary school difficult. Noah is bright and popular, but he has dyslexia which makes it tricky to keep up with the other students. Penny and Kat want to know if the Astrology Oracle can shed any light on anything that could help Noah navigate his next few years of school.

Penny's cards

Bottom Card

Meaning: What's On Your Mind? *Eleventh House*
The Eleventh House represents social connections, groups and teams, and may describe Noah's good relationships with friends at school, or his parents' buoyant social circle. The card of friendship is a positive sign that Noah and his family have a resourceful network of people willing to help.

Middle Left Card

Meaning: What Is There Too Much Of? *Tenth House*
The Tenth House is a card of traditional expectations, professionalism and ambitions. The 'too much' aspect of this card could relate to Penny and Kat feeling that the current structured schooling system isn't a good fit for Noah. The Tenth House's rigid rules could make Noah feel like a square peg in a round hole.

⋅+ ELEMENTAL SPREADS +⋅

Middle Right Card
Meaning: What Is There Too Little Of? *Copper*

The Copper Alchemical card promises transformation, and as this card corresponds with harmonious, sociable Venus, something beautiful is in the wings. Too little Copper suggests that Noah's family may underestimate the love that surrounds them. They may have experienced a lack of support or have not explored the network of positive connections that this card promises. Copper also promises a beautiful gift, but the gift has not yet been realized.

Top Card
Meaning: The Perfect Balance *Mars*

Mars is the card of speed, courage, strength and belief. Taking an independent stand is recommended now to readdress the balance in Penny, Kat and Noah's family. A feisty force for good, this card is bursting with raw potential, and Mars likes to shout and draw attention to injustice. Mars demands action, so Penny and Kat will discover that when they actively and positively explore new learning options for their son, they will be surprised how quickly they find their voice.

Conclusion for Penny

"This touched on something interesting for me because I'm not good at conflict. I knew that the problem was never with my son, but more the education system. There are outside groups that might be a help to Noah, but I haven't really introduced the idea to him because he has a lot of friends at school and doesn't want to seem like the odd one out. He's more developed socially and emotionally than most other kids of his age, and we need him to see that his neurodivergence is what makes him so brilliant. Maybe that's what the Copper card meant by a gift that's not been realized. I'm going to get more 'Mars' with Noah's teachers, I think because he's so bright in other ways that his dyslexia is being pushed under the carpet. Not anymore."

Elemental Water reading

When to use the Water layout
Use Water layouts when emotions are strong as this pattern of cards lends an emotional depth and perception to experiences of empathy, grief, friendship, heartache, and erotic connection.

Layout pattern
Four cards placed in a lucky horseshoe shape, as below.

Card position meanings:

Top Left Card
Meaning: The Source
While shuffling through your Astrology Oracle deck, empty your mind and let your instincts guide you to the card that shows where these feelings began for you or your querent. What circumstances led to this moment?

Bottom Left Card
Meaning: What Are You Holding On To?
Let your fingers guide you to the right card that gives clues as to what you, or the person you're reading for, is holding on to in this emotional situation. This card describes something that is needed or a situation that is stopping further growth.

Bottom Right Card
Meaning: What Can You Release?
Instinctively allow yourself to be guided to the card that describes what is done and dusted and needs to be set free.

Top Right Card
Meaning: Where Is Your Flow?
Find a card that shows how to leave or thrive in the current situation. Freedom, happiness and harmony mean you, or who you are reading for, can move into a fresher stream.

•+ ELEMENTAL SPREADS +•

Your example Water reading cards

For this example reading, imagine you are going through a difficult break-up. You have good people supporting you but you're finding it tough to imagine a new world where you'll find your joy again and move on with your life.

Top Left Card
Meaning: The Source *Aries*

The Aries card is a zodiac sign, so represents a person. The person in question is a natural leader, vibrant and full of enthusiasm. They are fun to be around, wear their heart on their sleeve, and fall in, and out, of love easily. This could describe the person you were in a relationship with, or a key person involved, possibly even yourself.

Bottom Left Card
Meaning: What Are You Holding On To? *Ninth House*

The Ninth House shows a willingness to broaden your horizons and being open to life's possibilities and challenges. It's an optimistic card that welcomes new discoveries and teaches you to embrace things that challenge you. In this position the Ninth House may show that you're holding onto a belief that the relationship opened you to different cultures and experiences, and that you don't want to lose that sense of adventure.

Bottom Right Card
Meaning: What Can You Release? *Saturday*

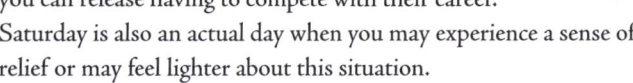

Saturday, named after Saturn, the most hard-working, ambitious planet focuses on business and earning money. It's a practical card, and in this position might suggest you worked together or had a business that is now out of your hands, which you may see as a blessing. Alternatively, your partner was too focused on work to make you happy, and you can release having to compete with their career. Saturday is also an actual day when you may experience a sense of relief or may feel lighter about this situation.

Top Right Card
Meaning: Where Is Your Flow? *Iron*

Iron is an Alchemical card that describes a transformational change in the way you feel about your current predicament. Courage is the message of this warrior card, trusting that you have what it takes to stick up for yourself and swim your way to clear waters. Your "flow," what will save you and give you a renewed sense of self, is your own strength and willingness to find a new sense of purpose. The changes coming may even push you into new territory emotionally and physically that soon put this heartache firmly in your past.

Elemental Water reading – Diane
(her/she), 65, Lancaster UK

Background
Diane feels unhappy with the way her life has turned out. She's been married for over 40 years, has two sons who have their own families. Although her husband has been a good father and a caring partner, she keeps wondering whether they should be doing something more adventurous with their lives.

Diane's cards

Top Left Card
Meaning: The Source *Copper*

Copper is a transformational Oracle Card that shows something lovely is on the horizon, and likely describes a talent for making her surroundings beautiful and harmonious. As the source of Diane's feelings, this could be a sign that in the beginning everything was rosy – she married for the right reasons and her life has been quite blessed with money, comfort and travel. It could be that the source of her feelings is that she's been a little too comfortable or under-challenged.

Bottom Left Card
Meaning: What Are You Holding On To? *Regulus*

As the Regulus card is associated with popularity, fame and success, maybe there's a certain amount of prestige surrounding Diane's current life that's hard to let go of. She could be well-respected, popular and social, and Diane might feel it's her duty to play up to her role as a respected member of her community.

Bottom Right Card

Meaning: What Can You Release? *Eleventh House*

Diane can release Eleventh House card associations, which are linked with groups, associations, teams and organizations. Diane may have built her identify through the groups and clubs she and her husband belong to but isn't happy to share how she really feels with the people around her. Releasing her need to keep up appearances circle could give her a new lease of life.

Top Right Card

Meaning: Where Is Your Flow? *First House*

The First House is Diane's identity and impressions she makes on others. It is clearly time for Diane to be herself, to enjoy her own interests, make her own friends and find out what she is passionate about. Her flow comes when she listens to her own voice, not her partner's or the opinions and interests of the groups around her.

Conclusion for Diane

"I found the reading a little uncomfortable. Yes, my life has been blessed in so many ways, so why am I now complaining? The reading made me think about whether I have been moulding myself around the people in my life, rather than being brave enough to be myself. It's only been in the last few years that I felt unhappy, but it's probably because I've not been living my own life – I've been doing what was expected of me for far too long, and I suppose it's time to find out who my real friends are."

Elemental Water reading – Douglas
(he/him), 33, Carmarthen, UK

Background

A year ago, Douglas discovered he has a health condition that will improve if he makes changes to his lifestyle. He's feeling unmotivated to get fit or give up any other bad habits and is constantly annoyed with himself for not being proactive. Douglas wants to know what emotions could be blocking his personal growth.

Douglas's cards

Top Left Card
Meaning: The Source *The Moon*

The Moon card explains that the source of Douglas's feelings comes from a very sensitive place. Deep attachment and longing are present in his inquiry, and great care needs to be taken not to hurt someone's sensitivities – possibly his own. Douglas may be feeling vulnerable and needs to be super kind to himself.

Bottom Left Card
Meaning: What Are You Holding On To? *Monday*

Monday is another Moon-based card, adding an extra layer of moony emotions to Douglas's current situation. Someone or something has a strong emotional hold on Douglas that may be keeping him from getting a clear idea of what he wants from life. Monday could also have significance for Douglas as a day when he realizes exactly what is holding him back, which will give him a clearer view on what's coming next.

ELEMENTAL SPREADS

Bottom Right Card
Meaning: What can you release? *Tenth House*
The Tenth House is the card of worldly success. Maybe Douglas needs to release his fear of failing, or not living up to others' opinions and expectations of him – real or imagined. The Tenth House also wants to take a traditional, tried and tested path, and to stick to rules and regulations, so to be free Douglas should set his own goals and guidelines.

Top Right Card
Meaning: Where is your flow? *Quicksilver*
This Alchemical Quicksilver card shows a shift in consciousness is going to happen and transform Douglas's future. Quicksilver, a liquid metal in the flow position, is an auspicious card for him, showing his attitude will change, and he'll become more flexible and adaptable. This card's association with clever planet Mercury reveals a love of words and conversation, and the more Douglas researches and talks about his situation the easier it will become. Talking about his situation will feel like therapy and he will become lighter and kinder to himself as he progresses.

Conclusion for Douglas
"There's some food for thought in there. I had a tough relationship with my mother who wasn't the most empathic person. She died before we had a chance to talk about it – and I'm not even sure I would have been brave enough to do that. I think that's left me feeling empty, or angry or something. And the cards are right in that I should be taking care of myself, instead of blaming her for not showing me how to do that. But I'm winning: I quit smoking three weeks ago after I found an online therapist."

The Card Meanings

·+ THE ASTROLOGY ORACLE +·

Astrology Oracle Cards

The Planets cards
The planets are the main players in your Astrology Oracle, and their symbolism is reflected throughout the entire deck.

The Zodiac Sign Cards
The Zodiac Signs represent different personality traits, attitudes and approaches to life, and when they appear in a reading, they usually symbolize people you know, or people you will soon meet who share the characteristics of that zodiac sign.

The House Cards
An astrology chart or horoscope is a circular map of the heavens that's split into 12 different areas of life, known as houses, where the energy of the planets and the personalities of the zodiac sign are played out and given more context.

Alchemical cards
The Alchemical cards are 12 astrological cards of special significance, 'wild' cards that are agents of change. You may have a stroke of unexpected good luck, sudden news, upheaval or an opportunity for transformation.

Days of the Week
There are seven Days of the Week cards, which as well as showing the actual days when things might happen, are also connected with different goddesses and gods. In ancient cultures each day was named after the planets they observed in the night sky.

The Sun

Key words: joy, growth, creativity, popularity

The Sun is a joyful card to see in any spread. Earth's nearest star is the bringer of life, illuminating all it touches with nurturing light and warmth. When The Sun turns up in a reading it shows a unique, creative force for the good, and reminds you to trust and connect with your own creativity through, visual arts, dancing, acting or any inspiring expressive endeavour. Warmth and generosity spill from this card's position in a layout, promising new life, birth and hopeful opportunities. The Sun also needs attention and blossoms in company and describes a desire for encouragement and praise. The Sun can feel lost or lonely if there's nobody to reflect its light and glory, so look to other cards to discover where support could come from. The Sun wants to make others happy and represents a willingness to bring happiness into the world. This is your time to shine!

The Moon

Key words: emotions, secrecy, instincts, attachment

The Moon card is linked to water and changing emotions, reflecting its constant pull on the restless tides. The Moon's changeable, reflective nature mirrors our own instinctual and emotional responses through its different phases and conditions. When The Moon card turns up in a reading, deep feelings are present, and caution should be taken not to hurt or provoke someone's sensitivities, which of course could be your own. Sensitive and impressionable, The Moon shows deep attachment and protective or defensive instincts – and a possibility that a secret is being kept. Intuition is key with this card, as it represents subconscious drives, habits and rhythms. It's a time to trust your feelings, even if they seem to lead you somewhere unexpected. If The Moon turns up in a reading, look to the surrounding cards to describe where the strong feelings are coming from and how to proceed for the best.

Mercury

Key words: versatility, communication, commerce, duplicity

MERCURY

Mercury represents the mind, thinking and communication. This card symbolizes a need to adapt and be flexible to changing circumstances, and a willingness to learn more. This is an excellent problem-solving card that describes clarity of mind and a cool-headed approach in dealing with any challenges. Learning new skills could be indicated and courses, classes and lessons could open new horizons, or lead to experiences that open your mind. Mercury appears when no one path is right or when there are many different options. The cards surrounding Mercury will give clues on how to proceed. Sometimes Mercury can indicate a trickster, someone who is trying to pull the wool over your eyes, a smooth talker or a charmer with dubious intentions. This is a good business card to see if you are asking the cards about a moneymaking venture - entrepreneurial and adaptable, Mercury shows a quick turnover and a beguiling way with words.

Venus

Key words: relationships, love, harmony, money

Fun, romance and enjoyment are big themes when harmonious, pleasure-loving Venus makes an appearance. Cooperation and partnership show the way forward, and love and relationships are high on the agenda. This is an excellent card to see if looking for guidance about a love affair or partnership, as it expresses a desire to be close to someone, or to work with others for a better outcome. Venus shows up when socializing and enjoyment are on the cards – a wonderful night out or a glamorous occasion, beautiful clothes, fun with friends, or a romantic trip can all be possible outcomes. If the cards were asked for guidance on a money matter, this is a fortunate planet to see. Money could be easily earned, or a gift could boost your bank balance. If Venus turns up in a reading about love, it's a sure sign that affection is deep and that feelings are returned, though the surrounding cards will give more information about the circumstances that will encourage love into your life, or the person you're reading for.

Mars

Key words: activity, courage, strength, passion

Mars is the planet of action, independence and will. When Mars appears in a reading it indicates strong passions and opinions. Frustration or anger needs healthy expression, and sexual relationships could sweep you off your feet. Impatience and spontaneity are present, and there could be a need to wait before making a move. A new relationship could be on the cards, but Mars tends to jump into new situations very quickly and needs to plan before committing to new ventures. Mars can show that you can't see the wood for the trees and need time or a shift in perspective before ploughing into a new situation. Decisions made now will be strong ones, and action will be heartfelt, but check you're not treading on someone else's toes before announcing plans for world domination. Mars represents vigorous good health and high energy levels, and the surrounding cards will give clues as to how to channel this feisty force for good.

Jupiter

Key words: luck, abundance, happiness, extravagance

Jupiter is the luckiest planet in astrology, and his presence in a reading is always a welcome sign. The bringer of optimism and hope, cheerful Jupiter turns mediocre projects into fabulous successes, and promises thought-provoking experiences such as travel, education, cultural and spiritual experiences. Jupiter expands awareness, which is why it's connected with meditation, religious experiences and a love of philosophy. This jovial planet card also describes a love of being outdoors, sport and the thrill of the open road, all of which could be a key factor in a reading. Jupiter's presence ensures a favourable outcome, and enjoyable times ahead, but it can also represent too much of a good thing – spending and budgets may go ignored, or over-indulging in food, drink or partying could create some problems – but there's no doubting the fun to be had in getting there. Look to surrounding cards to get a taste of where ebullient Jupiter will show its happy-go-lucky face.

+・ THE CARD MEANINGS ・+

Saturn

Key words: structure, tradition, ambition, reality

SATURN

The authoritative Saturn card shows up when experience, discipline, hard work and control should be seriously considered. Saturn also points to where you, or the person you're reading for, may have difficulties or feel like you're not good enough. Saturn has a serious influence and a bearing on our sense of purpose and direction, but this challenging planet also bestows the gift of time and teaches where we need to slow down and think through options carefully. Saturn can be a hard taskmaster, but when you meet his stern gaze head on, the rewards are long-lasting and filled with an unshakable sense of true achievement. Being organized, sticking to a structure and keeping a level head are all areas of life that Saturn has influence over, and, although these things might not be the most exciting or inspiring realities, without them life would be chaotic. Look to the other cards surrounding Saturn in your reading as these will describe areas of life in which you can succeed when you put in extra effort.

Aries

Key words: leader, courage, bossy,

The Aries card describes people who are brave, headstrong and a little bit childish. They love an adventure and charge at any obstacles in their path. They have a restless, vibrant energy and their enthusiasm is hard to resist. The Aries determination to succeed is legendary and makes them natural born leaders. Rams are independent creatures, and at work they like being the boss. Because they're the ones usually making the rules, they can find it difficult to take orders from people in authority. Your typical Aries is determined to get to the top of their chosen profession and is a spender rather than a saver, preferring short-term excitement to careful budgeting. Aries characters display the same dislike of commitment in relationships, even though they are passionate and fall in love easily. Learning to share and rely on others is challenging, but that's also what Aries finds most rewarding.

Taurus

Key words: dependable, patient, stubborn

Taurus people are noted for their dependability, patience and perseverance, and it's these qualities that often lead them to success. Their quiet strength and determination see these resilient characters thrive in difficult circumstances, as they take life as it comes, and deal calmly with situations that make others seem flaky. Taurus people are eternally trustworthy are faithful and stick up for loved ones even if they suspect they may be in the wrong. Taurus types are stubborn and not fond of change, and hate being rushed into making any hasty decisions. Their strongest desire is for personal security and a beautiful and harmonious home life. Their relationships are usually long-lasting and built on solid foundations because Taurus doesn't give their heart away easily. Taurus people are slow to make decisions but once they make up their minds, they'll doggedly pursue their goal until they reach it. Taurus needs to learn to embrace change as potentially liberating and life-enhancing, rather than something to be feared.

Gemini

Key words: intellectual, quick-thinking, moody

Geminis are curious, quick-witted and light-hearted. They're named after the twins Castor and Pollux in Greek mythology because they can display two very different sides to their personality – cheerful and upbeat one minute then seething and withdrawn the next. Geminis can juggle many projects simultaneously and thrive in new surroundings and circumstances. With many friends and acquaintances, Gemini types enjoy learning and sharing new information. These loquacious characters are the most gifted communicator in the zodiac, with excellent writing and speaking ability. Gemini people pick up new languages fast and make excellent salespeople who enjoy variety and thrive wherever there are plenty of people to talk to. Gemini types can be incurable flirts, with their romantic lives being as colourful as their taste in clothes. They have a natural gift for finding something in common with even the most difficult of people. Gemini people often have butterfly minds, which prevents them from getting too deeply connected with the world around them, but when they focus their brilliance on one area of life, they are transformed.

Cancer

Key words: empathetic, nurturing, sensitive

Cancer individuals are tenacious, caring and immensely protective of the people they care about. Like the hard shell of the crab, they project a tougher exterior than they have, to hide their sensitive natures. Cancer people's emotions are as changeable as the phases of their ruling planet, the Moon, and these empathic personalities are perceptive and shockingly intuitive. The Cancer person's nature sees them excel as carers, cooks and teachers and they make for loyal, loving partners. Cancer people are shrewd with money and have excellent business instincts, and their tenacious appetites mean they make formidable opponents.

When they have what they want in their pincers, it's very difficult to convince them to give it up, even if it's no longer useful to them. Cancer is the hoarder of the zodiac because they are sentimental about any possession that holds a special memory. Cancer people need to let go and trust that everything will be okay, even if they're not in control.

Leo

Key words: flamboyant, generous, creative

Ruled by the creative life-force of the Sun, Leo characters need to feel they're at the centre of the Universe, with a strong need to light up and energize the people around them. These proud, flamboyant people crave attention and feel diminished without an adoring audience, but it is easy to warm to Leo's open and generous spirit. Creative and organized with big-cat authority, a typical Leo can become bossy with the people they care about but insist this is the only way to get their rightful opinions heard. In romance, a Leo needs to feel like they are the centre of the Universe and needs to feel adored, but Leo types are more easily hurt than most people realize, and even constructive criticism can be taken as a blow to their ego. However, when a Leo feels loved and trusted they will move mountains to please the people they care about. Leo people need to learn to have confidence in themselves as individuals, and to feel like they are enough on their own merit.

Virgo

Key words: organized, capable, critical

Virgos are the busiest sign in the zodiac with an inexhaustible To Do List. If you want something done, ask a Virgo and if they can't do it, they'll know someone who can. Neat, tidy and organized, these down-to-earth, capable characters like to sort out a mess. Virgo people are full of excellent advice but in their pursuit of perfection they can sometimes appear critical, when they're just trying to help you be the best you can be. Virgo types are modest and even shy with strangers, but once they feel relaxed in your company, you'll discover they have a strong opinion on everything, and their intelligent well-thought arguments can be extremely persuasive. In love Virgos are thoughtful, kind and patient, though they need to learn to relax and let the small things take care of themselves.

Libra

Key words: artistic, fair, indecisive

Librans strive for harmony in all areas of their lives. Refined and charming, Libra love to please and learn from the people around them. They are skilled diplomats who can't bear unfairness, but they often avoid conflict in their private lives. Left to their own devices, these charming, intelligent individuals can take an age to make important decisions, so it's essential for them to find someone to bat ideas back and forth with to help them understand themselves and their lives better. Libra characters have a flair for decoration, are skilled crafts people, or have an excellent taste in art or music. Because romance and relationships are so important to a typical Libra, it can also be a tough testing ground, as their expectations of their partners are high. Learning to enjoy their own company and taking a more independent stand is difficult for Libra people, but finding their own voice is richly rewarding.

Scorpio

Key words: intuitive, insightful, secretive

Scorpio people draw from deep pools of emotional and physical energy and need to find a positive outlet for their intense feelings. Usually good with money, Scorpios don't waste their resources on fripperies, but they can become obsessive collectors. At work Scorpios push themselves and enjoy a challenge, the more daunting the better. They can be demanding and secretive but also very rewarding romantic partners. It can be difficult to hide under a Scorpio's constant scrutiny, but Scorpio is one of the most loyal signs of the zodiac. Power games can arise if jealousies are stirred, and that's when the legendary Scorpio 'stinger' is most likely to make an appearance. But if you have a Scorpio's trust, you'll have a deeply intuitive, insightful and loyal partner or friend. When Scorpio people let down their defences and show the world that they too are vulnerable, they attract the respect and support they crave.

Sagittarius

Key words: adventurous, independent, restless

Sagittarius people are freedom-loving spirits who thrive on challenge and adventure. These generous, outgoing characters have an infectiously enthusiastic approach to life and can become bored when expected to respect customs or obey rules and regulations. These larger-than-life types don't know the meaning of moderation, which can have a punishing effect on their bank accounts, but they rarely let such minor inconveniences get in the way of their grand plans. Because of their fear of being stifled or restricted, a typical Sagittarius needs a broad-minded, inspiring partner who will understand their innate restlessness and try to keep their relationship fresh and exciting. Sagittarius needs to remember that the grass isn't always greener on the other side, but that's tough for someone whose love of travel pushes them to continually expand their comfort zone.

Capricorn

Key words: ambitious, practical, funny

Patient, determined and always realistic, Capricorn people don't rush into anything. They have a cool, logical approach to life and take pride in adopting practical, measurable plans to achieve their aims. Slowly and patiently your typical Capricorn will reach the top of their chosen profession. They're not flashy, loud or boastful, but they are winners with quiet, disciplined confidence. Capricorn characters usually have tight control over their emotions, which can make them seem a little distant. But underneath that composed exterior is a loyal, devoted character who will try to move mountains for the right person and once you get to know them, the average Capricorn has a wickedly dry sense of humour. Capricorns could make their life easier by remembering that happiness and worldly success are not always the same thing, but it is difficult for these ambitious, business-savvy over achievers to rest on their laurels.

Aquarius

Key words: just, eccentric, rebellious

Eccentric, inventive Aquarius people can come across as a little bit "out there" or ahead of their time. Quirky and aloof, Aquarius people are unpredictable but are always friendly. Humanitarian and sociable, Aquarians feel at home with many varied groups of people, and their insatiable curiosity about others is one of their most endearing qualities, though they can find it difficult to relate to people on a deeper, more emotional level. They have a rebellious, independent quality that keeps them a little separate from others, but they're the first to offer help in a crisis, or just when you need a friend. Aquarius is most at home in any group, club or collective, and they're the first to introduce you to people with similar interests. Although they can be sentimental and surprisingly romantic, Aquarians need to appreciate that their own, and others' emotions, cannot always be rationalized or explained intellectually.

Pisces

Key words: unpredictable, mystical, imaginative

Pisces people are gentle, compassionate and understanding. Pisces have a dual nature, so can seem happy and optimistic one minute and grumpy or discontented the next. Wonderfully artistic and imaginative, Pisces prefers to escape the banality of the real world into music, theatre, art and poetry. These empathic people seem connected to others on a psychic level that goes beyond words, and they excel at expressing their innermost feelings to the people they love. Natural philosophers and poets, Pisces seems wise beyond their years and just being in their silent company can feel healing and restorative. Pisces take their secrets to the grave and this deep trust earns them forever friends who never forget their kindness. Pisceans need to learn that when they ignore difficult situations, they might have to deal with even more confusing consequences later.

First House

Rules: self-image, identity, character, ego

The First House is known as the House of Self because when it turns up in a reading it symbolizes a fresh start in how your express yourself to the world. This card reflects your outward personality, the first impression you make, and your core sense of self. The First House card can also describe your physical appearance – your overall look, body type and style choices. When you see this card in a reading it asks you to look at your personality – your core traits, strengths and weaknesses. Your self-image might be impacted, and you might want to question how you see yourself or how you compare yourself to other people. Your vitality, energy levels and physical health are brought to the fore, and the surrounding cards will give more information about who you feel you are, inside and out.

THE CARD MEANINGS

Second House

Rules: money, talents, values, self-worth

If the Second House oracle card appears in a spread, your values, possessions, and financial resources are under review. Your relationship with material possessions, money and self-worth is highlighted and reveals your financial habits, spending patterns and attitude towards abundance. This oracle card also touches on your talents and abilities to generate income. You are being asked to think about how you feel about the things you own, and which possessions really matter to you. Are you happy about the way you spend your cash? Is your money working for you? Are you enjoying earning, or is it a chore? Your self-worth is also questioned here, and you're being advised to question whether you are being paid enough for your services. The spotlight is on your talents and skills, and how you use them to get the most enjoyment from life.

Third House

Rules: intellect, communication, thinking, conversation

Your mind, communication style and local environment are illuminated when the Third House card makes an appearance. This card also represents siblings, neighbours and short-distance travel. How you speak to other people, and how they talk to you, is being examined, as is how quickly you learn from other people. The way you choose to express yourself through your conversation style, listening ability and willingness to share information is being examined with this card, and it shows a need to learn more, or that more information is needed. Flexibility is needed when this card shows up, either to adapt to new circumstances or to accommodate other people's different opinions. Being open-minded and finding ways to stay interested in something could be important, and discovering methods to get information across more effectively could open new doors and possibilities. This card can also mean you're over-analyzing a situation or have information overload and need to understand something in bite-sized chunks.

Fourth House

Rules: home, family, nurturing, security

This card signifies your home, family and emotional security. When this card appears in a spread it shows that your roots and your past are being examined. Your early years, the emotional baggage you still carry and your sense of belonging in your current environment can be explored. Childhood experiences could be linked to how you're feeling now, whether these are positive or negative, and your relationship with your mother may reveal some interesting observations. Your inner sense of security, or insecurity is being examined, and old fears or anxieties may be on your mind. The Fourth House card also shows the best way to nurture yourself, how to take care of your inner child. Having inner strength and belief is important now, and the cards that surround the Fourth House will give clues as to what will make you feel safe, loved and held. Caring for others could be the theme of a spread that shows this oracle card, whether it's you that needs looking after, or you're caring for someone else.

Fifth House

Rules: love affairs, creativity, gambling, popularity

Self-expression, love and creativity are the focus of this card. It represents romance, children and hobbies. How do you play and have fun? Are you expressing your creative side? The Fifth House encourages you to embrace your inner child and experience joy – to find yourself and enjoy being yourself. This card appears in a reading when you need to express your talents and entertain others. You want to be admired, and to return your love in kind. Romance and love affairs could be on the horizon, or an existing happy relationship may take a happy turn for the better. Your popularity is strong, and your confidence impresses others who may be happy for you to lead the way in a particular situation. This Fifth House may also show up in a spread when a risk or gamble can be considered, and the surrounding cards will help you to decide the outcome.

Sixth House

Rules: health, routine work, pets, organisation

Your daily life, health and work are highlighted in this card. It represents your habits, routines, and being of service to others. Pay attention to your physical and mental well-being. Are you taking care of yourself? The Sixth House governs your daily routines: health, habits and your work environment, and asks that you pay attention to your daily patterns and how you care for your physical and mental well-being. The Sixth House oracle card encourages a balanced approach to life, emphasizing the importance of attention to detail – how you eat, your sleeping, daily exercise and how your job affects your anxiety levels. This is a practical card that shows a need to tidy up, make lists and get organized. Chaos can now be turned into clear paths, simple ideas and self-nurturing practices that make a big difference in the long term. Pets and animals also come under the Sixth House influence, with their presence being either stressful or providing welcome love and structure in the form of daily responsibility.

Seventh House

Rules: relationships, others, partnerships, love

The Seventh House card illuminates your relationships with other people, particularly romantic partnerships. Love is in the air, and whether you're married or single and looking for love, this card appears when romance needs consideration. Depending on the surrounding oracle cards, it may be time to rethink the balance in your relationships and address the dynamic. If looking for love, this card is an excellent sign that someone interesting is on the horizon, or that your love is returned, but it may be that the person who loves you cannot be with you for reasons that may be depicted on the surrounding cards. The Seventh House shows that others are on your side, and that you have support for any venture you are about to take on. Business partners are also covered by this card, and working with other people should be harmonious. Love is real now, reach out to others as their support will be given willingly.

Eighth House

Rules: transformation, beginnings and endings, power, secrets

The Eighth House oracle card speaks of endings, new beginnings and transformations. Sometimes a crisis occurs that means you must take action, and this card shows that you are either at the end of one cycle or are at an exciting crossroads, about to take a step into the unknown. The Eighth House also represents secrets. Depending on the type of spread and surrounding cards, a secret may come out, or you may be asked to keep something to yourself. There is power in this card, and you may have more influence over a situation than you think you do. Others may trust you more than you realize, but their faith in you might not be obvious to you. If you're going through a difficult time the appearance of the Eighth House could bring hope of a transformation – that your challenges are shaping you to emerge from the depths stronger, wiser and better prepared to face any hardship.

Ninth House

Rules: travel, education, faith, philosophy

The Ninth House invites you to broaden your horizons and seek knowledge. This broad-minded oracle card encourages you to embrace and merge with different cultures, to learn new skills and have an adventurous approach to life. Keeping a sense of perspective is important now as you could blow something out of proportion. Be optimistic, and approach new challenges as learning curves that will take you to undreamed-of heights. Philosophy is also covered by the Ninth House, and discovering new perspectives on life could be a game-changer. You might become interested in different faiths or religious beliefs and explore your own spirituality. Open yourself to life's adventures and possibilities – step out your comfort zone and embrace not knowing what is ahead. A chance to travel may be on the cards, and could indicate a wonderful adventure ahead. The Ninth House is usually a welcome sign of freedom on the horizon.

Tenth House

Rules: worldly success, career, public self, ambitions

Your ambitions can be reached when the Tenth House appears in a spread. Your hard work pays off and your goals in your professional life are in the spotlight. Your reputation glows, and you become popular at work. This card also encourages you to build a stable foundation for your future. You can see the way ahead clearly and are in a practical frame of mind that helps you build slowly but surely on your success. The Tenth House card doesn't build on pie-in-the-sky ideas, it promises to get you to the top of your mountain, but only if you stick to the rules and don't take shortcuts. Taking a sensible tried-and-tested approach to any challenges will be a sure winner. Also represented by the Tenth House is your relationships with your father, your boss or people you look up to. Someone you respect could offer help that launches you in a new direction.

Eleventh House

Rules: friends, groups, movements, socialising

The Eleventh House oracle card represents your social life – your friends, colleagues, teammates and the groups you belong to. New friends are on the horizon, people who will make a positive difference to your life, who will bolster your confidence and help you achieve your dreams. A humanitarian card, the Eleventh House shows where you can make a difference to other people's lives by joining charitable organizations, political movements or groups who work together for the common good. You may make new friends with people who share your passions and interests, or join a company where your co-workers become your best friends. This friendly oracle card asks you to surround yourself with like-minded people and interesting characters because you'll discover a goldmine of useful information. Don't try to go it alone – wherever this card turns up in a reading, it's time to work with others, and to learn from their experience. It's a great time to seek inspiration and encouragement.

THE CARD MEANINGS

Twelfth House

Rules: dreams, unconscious, fantasies, intuition

The Twelfth House is the most mysterious and introspective of the houses. It represents your subconscious mind, what's going on with you at a deeper level that you might not even be aware of. When this card makes itself known in a spread you are being asked to pay attention to your dreams, as repeating patterns or themes could give you more insight into whatever you are reading the cards to help you with. Your fantasies can also help now – as even the most outlandish ones reveal what motivates you, or give ideas as to what would make you happiest. The Twelfth House oracle card appears when you may need to disconnect with what's going on around you, and spend time alone to centre yourself. Depending on the surrounding cards, you must follow your instincts and intuition now, as these aspects of yourself are strongly trying to point you in the right direction if you listen.

The Comet

Key thought: something new

The sighting of a comet used to be a harbinger of events that would change the divine order of the world, and The Comet oracle card represents the things in life you don't have any control over. Change can be scary, daunting, wonderful or baffling, but when you see The Comet card – it's coming. It's hard to prepare for something unexpected, so the Comet card asks that you don't catastrophize before you know what's going to happen. You may have an inkling of something in the pipeline, but The Comet is usually not predictable – it's something that takes your world by storm for better or worse. Upheaval can be liberating, tearing you away from habits that aren't doing you much good, or showing you that a better life than you'd ever imagined can be born now. Even a disruptive, or shocking, event can force a jolt of consciousness to awaken a new perspective, and you could discover that you're much better off than you thought.

Caduceus

Key thought: peace and protection

CADUCEUS

The Caduceus is a healing oracle card that announces communication, help, healing and balance. You must work together now to bring your hopes and desires to fruition, whether this is through striking a truce with someone or working with like-minded people for the greater good. Maybe you need to be kinder to yourself by making peace with the past or give yourself permission to be exactly as you are. There's a guardian influence when the Caduceus appears, showing you that a higher power is guiding you through a difficult time, and though you may feel anxious, everything is working itself out on another level of consciousness. Like the entwined serpents depicted on the card the Caduceus shows the duality of life and need to find harmony in tough times. Your powers of diplomacy can also be used to act as a go-between to soothe troubled waters between people you care about.

Rahu

Key thought: your lesson to learn

Rahu is a point in an astrological chart that represents where you long to be in life. Rahu is the true north and indicates the areas of growth and development you're meant to explore. It's like a compass pointing towards your destiny, guiding you towards new experiences and personal transformation. You may feel a sense of incompleteness that the Rahu oracle card acknowledges while offering to help you find your way. The path ahead may be full of obstacles but, without them, reaching your goal wouldn't be satisfying. This karmic card is showing you what you need to learn to evolve - sometimes this feels like the mistake you continually repeat until you finally get it. A repeating pattern in relationships, for example, a tendency to spend all your money or finding it difficult to look after your health. Rahu can bring challenges and obstacles, but these offer a chance to break the negative habits and offer opportunities for growth and transformation. The Rahu oracle card shows where you can face your fears and overcome limitations and describes the lessons you must learn to become who you long to be.

Ketu

Key thought: your lesson to teach

Ketu is a point in the birth chart, the counterpart oracle card to Rahu, and describes what you already know, or learned in previous lifetimes. The natural talents and abilities you take for granted, or have never questioned, just feel like a natural part of who you are because they were never a struggle. You might be a gregarious person where others can't find their voice, a natural athlete, when others spend years building their strength, or have an inborn knack for making money, where others lack the confidence to attract business. But you may undervalue the things you're skilled in or dismiss them as being unworthy because you didn't find them challenging. You might not even be aware that you're naturally talented in some areas because you didn't experience much resistance. This oracle card brings your natural talents to light, and describes the lessons you teach others, consciously or not.

Regulus

Key thought: Fame

REGULUS

Regulus, the brightest star in the constellation of Leo, is considered a 'royal' star that symbolizes leadership, ambition and courage. The Regulus oracle card is linked with fame, honour, and success and describes shining talents and times when you're at the very top of your game. You are capable of achievements that could make a name for yourself and your drive for success is strong. Its presence might indicate a period of increased visibility or a new leadership role, or it could signal a time for being ruthlessly creative and pursuing ambitious goals. There is also a need for careful consideration of the impact of your actions on others, as your may have more power and influence than you realize. You must make responsible decisions now and step into your power while remaining grounded and humble. Regulus's appearance is a call to use your influence for the greater good and to lead with compassion.

+• THE CARD MEANINGS •+

Gold

Key thought: abundance

Linked with the generosity and splendour of the Sun, when you see this noble card during a consultation it is a potent symbol of abundance, prosperity and success. The Gold card represents the alchemical goal of perfection and enlightenment – the highest state of awareness and wisdom. A period of manifestation and reward for your hard work and dedication could be on the cards, and good luck may come in the form of a windfall, a pay rise or a sudden period of happiness. Your creative ideas may go down better than you expect, you feel popular and happy and will enjoy being in the spotlight. The recognition you receive when this card makes an appearance will you feel more generous and loving, and sharing your blessings makes you feel more grateful for your wins. It's time to enjoy your success while giving something back to society.

Silver

Key thought: reflection

Emotional depth is this oracle card's strength as it is linked with the feeling, responsive nature of the Moon in astrology. The alchemical symbolism of Silver represents the principles of inner wisdom, contemplation and reflection, and the malleable qualities of this yielding metal correspond with its impressionable, sensitive attributes. This mysterious card encourages introspection and self-care, and a need to be gentle with yourself. You may need to balance your inner thoughts, assumptions and longings with what's going on in the outer world as your feelings could be magnified. The purity linked with the Silver card means your feelings could be intense and clear – and it's possible you may overreact to something that doesn't deserve your attention. This may be a time to contemplate where you want to be in life, to process your thoughts and feelings in readiness to move on from past hurts.

Quicksilver

Key thought: the shapeshifter

When the Quicksilver card appears in your oracle pack reading, it's a sure sign that you can adapt or thrive in any new situation. Naturally associated with the planet Mercury, the nimblest, cleverest planet in the zodiac, Quicksilver's presence means that your words are the key to success – you can talk your way through any challenges and charm and entertain your way to success. Quicksilver is a symbol linked with transformative processes as it transmutes from a solid state to liquid and even a gas. You are flexible, clever and more resilient than you may think, and your quick wit and creative ideas bring a smile to the stoniest of faces. If you're worried about having to give a good account of yourself in a presentation, interview or even a first date – this card promises success. The Quicksilver card also warns of anyone trying to pull the wool over your eyes, or of someone pretending to be something they are not.

Copper

Key thought: something beautiful

COPPER

Copper is linked with the planet Venus, representing love, beauty and desire. When this lovely card turns up in a spread, something delightful is waiting in the wings. Your social life may open, bringing a new romantic relationship, helpful friends and like-minded souls who bring light and laughter into your day. In alchemical symbolism, copper is associated with pleasure, refined good taste and sensuality, and its malleability shows the ability to shape your surroundings. You have excellent taste now and can improve your living space and bring harmony to the people you share it with. The Copper card asks you to connect with what you love most, to build bridges with people you've fallen out with and to appreciate those who bring you the most happiness. Money, gifts, a romantic encounter or a trip of a lifetime are possible now, as are praise, an ego-boosting flirtation, or extra cash to spend on luxuries.

Iron

Key thought: courage

You're a rock in a storm when the Iron oracle card shows itself. Whatever the challenges ahead, you're prepared for them. There could be a battle you have to face, but you have the energy to do it and might even enjoy having to stick up for yourself. In alchemical symbolism, iron is associated with the planet Mars, representing strength, courage, and willpower. Iron is the metal of the warrior, symbolizing both physical and psychological challenges. Courage isn't always obvious, so if you're struggling with inner turmoil or unwelcome thoughts, you have the right set of tools to dismantle any negativity or anxiety. The Iron card also signifies impulsiveness, so a balanced approach rather than putting all your eggs in one basket will work better for you now. You're full of raw potential now and need to channel your energy into something positive, otherwise you'll feel restless or will create friction just to get a reaction.

Tin

Key thought: lucky you

The Tin oracle card is always a welcome sight. Connected with fortunate, expansive Jupiter in astrology, the alchemical symbolism of Tin represents the bridge between the earthly and celestial realms and the potential for human greatness. A stoke of good luck will appear in your life, creating sudden possibilities and a path to something you long for. You may experience a chance meeting with someone who gives you valuable information or points you in a new direction. An unexpected windfall or gift could help you turn a tricky corner, or a love affair may sweep you off your feet. Good news after hard times puts a smile back on your face, or a new job appears exactly when you need it. Tin luck usually appears out of the blue, but it can also represent a lucky talent that is already within you and needs expressing.

Lead

Key thought: beginnings and endings

In alchemical symbolism, lead is associated with the planet Saturn, representing limitation, structure, and time. It is seen as the base metal, the starting point of the alchemical process. The Lead oracle card is linked to your physical body, mortality, and the challenges of the human condition. It asks you to take you and your well-being seriously, to create good habits, be practical and to follow sensible advice. Seeing the Lead oracle card in a reading advises you to listen to guidance from experienced people who care about you – even if you don't much like what they have to say. It's time to pull your metaphorical socks up and place some structure back into your life. The Lead card's appearance also reminds you of the tremendous power and potential within you. You have everything you need to break free from limitations – so keep trying. If you fail – get back up and try again until you get there.

Monday

Planet: moon

Monday comes from "Moon's Day". The Latin name for moon is *luna* and in French, Monday is still called *Lundi*. As the Moon is associated with intuition, emotions and feelings, this Day of the Week card shows up in a consultation when emotions are a key part of the reading. Your moods might be up and down and you're sensitive to others' feelings. The Monday card can show the seeds of a new romance, or feelings for someone that can't be openly expressed. Monday can also relate to people in your care, or are responsible for. Monday, with its connection to the impressionable Moon, shows artistic talents and expressive skills that you may be keeping to yourself out of shyness. It's time to stop daydreaming and show the world what you're capable of – maybe even next Monday. The day of Monday could be when something is going to happen or maybe has already happened the previous Monday, but the day itself will assume special significance.

Tuesday

Planet: Mars

TUESDAY

The origin of the word Tuesday originates from the Germanic god of war – Tiu, or Tiw, which morphed into English as "Tiwsday" and, eventually, Tuesday. In French, Tuesday is *Mardi*, derived from Mars, the Roman god of war and agriculture (Tiw's equivalent). The Tuesday card is strong and fearless, and often shows that action needs to be taken. Machines, cars and computers relate to the Tuesday card, and you work on this day better as an independent force, or as your own boss, rather than working in a team. You might be feeling impatient for someone to make a move, answer a question or you could just be feeling restless and a little temperamental. Your temper is hot, but your anger is brief and spectacular, and you soon regain composure. The Tuesday card's appearance can also show the significance of the day itself, so look to surrounding cards to work out why Tuesday might be of special significance.

Wednesday

Planet: mercury

The Latin for Wednesday is *dies Mercurii* – day of Mercury – which comes from the Germanic name *Wōdnesdæg* or day of Odin, who was the equivalent god to Mercury. The Wednesday card is a welcome sign that means your ideas are bright, and that you will receive words of wisdom from friends or loved ones. There might be two sides to this story, or you could be in two minds about how you want to move forward. Wednesday can sometimes mean you don't have all the information you need to make the right decision – and the surrounding cards should give you a better idea about how to move forward. You have the gift of the gab now, and are encouraged to make new friends and learn from the people around you. It's an excellent time to begin a new class or work with others on an interesting project, and you can juggle many different tasks.

•+ THE CARD MEANINGS +•

Thursday

Planet: jupiter

THURSDAY

Thursday originates from the old English name, *Thundresdaeg* – day of thunder – named after the god Thor, who in Latin was known as Jovis (Jupiter). The Thursday oracle card almost always sends a positive message. This jolly cards show that it's time to make a big impact and to believe in yourself. Be generous and optimistic in your outlook and don't dwell on any negatives. This lucky card encourages you to accept opportunities and push for bigger, better and more extravagant deals and projects. This is not a time to be shy about showing off your skills and talents – the world needs your wisdom and experience – and you should give it willingly. Exciting trips, holidays and celebrations are on the cards, and you want everyone to have a good time. The only downside of Thursday is that you could blow your budget or indulge in too much of a good thing. Thursday should also be considered as a day of the week when good news, enjoyment and extravagance is on the agenda.

Friday

Planet: venus

Friday is the Old English "day of Frigg" who was the Norse goddess of fertility and love. The Latin/Roman equivalent is Venus, and her Greek counterpart is Aphrodite. When the Friday oracle appears in your consultation, romance, friendship and artistic pursuits are areas to explore. Harmony and equality in relationships is important for this people-pleasing card, and its appearance in a spread could indicate a longing for romance, even if you're in a happy partnership. You want to feel like you're special, and to be treated accordingly. Your relationship with fairness and judgment are to be explored, whether you're being fair to someone else, or if they're judging you harshly. The Friday card can appear when you need to take an independent stand, and stand on your own two feet, because this card dislikes conflict and shies away from it, when you're in the right. The Friday card can also be taken literally as events that may happen on that day depending on the surrounding cards.

Saturday

Planet: saturn

Saturday is the planet Saturn's day, named after the Latin *Sāturnī*, which led to the Old English pronunciation and spelling *Saternesdæg* followed by the Middle English *Saturdai* before English speakers settled on Saturday. The Saturday card appears when work, ambitions and business are to be examined. A slow, sensible approach to new people or situations is encouraged, as trust needs to be earned, and a practical approach to life is favoured. There is money to be earned when the Saturday card appears, and you'll be able to achieve your highest aspirations, but only if you're committed, patient and learn from your mistakes. A father figure, your boss or a teacher could impart a valuable lesson now, or you may be the one taking on extra responsibilities and leading the way for others. Saturday can also literally be the day that something significant happens, depending on the surrounding cards.

Sunday

Planet: sun

SUNDAY

The name for Sunday stems from the Middle English word *sunnenday*, which is a derivation from the Latin *diēs sōlis* or "Sun's day". The Sunday oracle card illuminates any reading with light and life-giving creativity. The message here is that you are more powerful than you realize, and that no matter what the challenges, you'll find a way through. The Saturday card shows that you have support, and that other people trust you. The message is to be yourself, don't feel you have to change or pretend to be someone else – you are enough. Your natural talents shine through, and you may become very popular, but being in the limelight may also attract some unhelpful comments or undeserved criticism. You want everyone to love you now, so gossip or negative comments may sting more than usual, but remember your fans far outweigh your detractors. The Sunday card can also refer to the actual day when something significant happens.

Index of cards

1. The Sun 77
2. The Moon 78
3. Mercury 79
4. Venus 80
5. Mars 81
6. Jupiter 82
7. Saturn 83
8. Aries 84
9. Taurus 85
10. Gemini 86
11. Cancer 87
12. Leo 88
13. Virgo 89
14. Libra 90
15. Scorpio 91
16. Sagittarius 92
17. Capricorn 93
18. Aquarius 94
19. Pisces 95
20. First House 96
21. Second House 97
22. Third House 98
23. Fourth House 99
24. Fifth House 100
25. Sixth House 101
26. Seventh House 102
27. Eighth House 103
28. Ninth House 104
29. Tenth House 105
30. Eleventh House 106
31. Twelfth House 107
32. The Comet 108
33. Caduceus 109
34. Rahu 110
35. Ketu 111
36. Regulus 112
37. Gold 113
38. Silver 114
39. Quicksilver 115
40. Copper 116
41. Iron 117
42. Tin 118
43. Lead 119
44. Monday 120
45. Tuesday 121
46. Wednesday 122
47. Thursday 123
48. Friday 124
49. Saturday 125
50. Sunday 126